Music From Four Centuries

For String Orchestra

Transcribed
by
Samuel Applebaum

Table of Contents

	Page
MENUET — G. F. Handel (1685-1759)	4
MOODS — B. Bartók (1881-1945)	14
SARABANDE — K. Böhm (1844-1920)	6
SERENADE FOR STRINGS — W. A. Mozart (1756-1791)	2
SONATINA FOR STRINGS — M. Clementi (1752-1832)	11
TO A WILD ROSE — E. MacDowell (1861-1908)	10
TWO HUNGARIAN FOLK TUNES — B. Bartók (1881-1945)	8

Copyright © 1992 CPP/Belwin, Inc.
15800 N.W. 48th Avenue, Miami FL. 33014
International Copyright Secured   Made In U.S.A.   All Rights Reserved

Serenade for Strings

W. A. MOZART
*Transcribed for String Orchestra
by Samuel Applebaum*

> Use the **martelé** stroke on the quarter notes marked with dots. The notes marked with dots and dashes are to be played **détaché lancé**, which is a smooth stroke with a slight pause after the note has been played. Use the **spiccato** bowing on all 8th notes marked with dots.
>   At each **comma**, leave a slight pause for phrasing, with the bow remaining on the string.
> // The **two slanted lines** mean that the bow is to be lifted from the string.
> o-o This **means that you are** to look up at the conductor. This sign is used in professional symphony orchestras.
> ▫ The small **square notes** indicate that the finger is to be placed on two strings. This square note is to be stopped **by the fingers** but not played. It makes it possible to go on from one string to another smoothly.
>   In the 1st measure lift the bow at the slanted lines and bring it quickly to the frog, in order to play the 8th notes up-bow using the spiccato bowing.

Copyright © 1965, 1991 (Assigned) CPP/BELWIN, INC.

32
spicc.
below middle
cresc.
ff
38
f
(or)
p
42
46
dim.
51
mf
55
58
62
67
spicc.

Menuet

GEORGE F. HÄNDEL
*Transcribed for String Orchestra
by Samuel Applebaum*

> **Use the martelé stroke** on the quarter notes marked with dots, **and** the spiccato stroke on the 8th notes marked with dots. The notes marked with dots and dashes are to be played détaché lancé, which is a smooth stroke with a slight pause after the note has been played.
> **At each comma,** leave a slight pause for phrasing, with the bow remaining on the string.
> // **The two slanted** lines mean that the bow is to be lifted from the string.
> ○─○ **This means that** you are to look up at the conductor. This sign is used in professional symphony orchestras.
> ◻ **The small square** notes indicate that the finger is to be placed on two strings. This square note is to be **stopped by the** fingers but not played. It makes it possible to go on from one string to another smoothly.

57
61
spicc.
66
dim.
spicc.
69
74
dim.
77
81
85
dim.
89
93
97
dim.e.rit.
a tempo
101
109
113
harmonic on the A string
117
rit.

Sarabande

CARL BOHM
*Transcribed for String Orchestra
by Samuel Applebaum*

// The two slanted lines mean that you are to lift the bow from the string. Start down-bow on the next note.

∞ This means that you are to look up at the conductor. This sign is used in professional symphony orchestras.

The small square notes indicate that the finger is to be placed on two strings. This square note is to be stopped by the fingers but not played. It makes it possible to go from one string to another smoothly.

Use the spiccato bowing on the eighth notes marked with dots.

7

Two Hungarian Folk Tunes

BELA BARTOK
Transcribed for String Orchestra
by Samuel Applebaum

// The two slanted lines mean that you are to lift the bow from the string. Start down-bow on the next note.
⚯ This means that you are to look up at the conductor. This sign is used in professional symphony orchestras.
The notes marked with a dot and a dash are to be played détaché lancé— a slight pause between each note without the martelé accent. Use the spiccato bowing on all the eighth notes marked with dots.

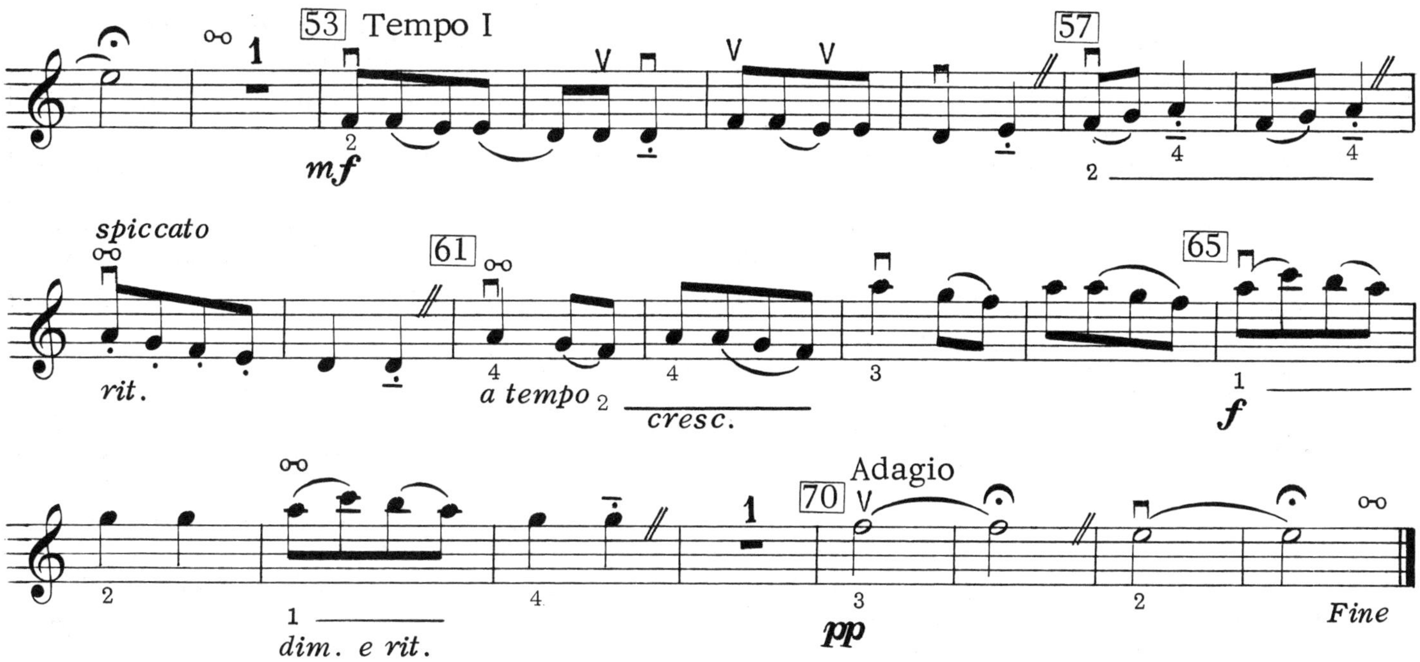
53 Tempo I
57
mf
spiccato
61
65
rit.
a tempo
cresc.
f
Adagio
70
dim. e rit.
pp
Fine

II.

Andante (♩ = 63)
5
9
13
(Cello, Bass melody)
17
Adagio
24
p
mf
pp
D. C. No. 1 al Fine

To A Wild Rose

EDWARD MACDOWELL
*Transcribed for String Orchestra
by Samuel Applebaum*

// The two slanted lines mean that you are to lift the bow from the string. Start down-bow on the next note.

∞ This means that you are to look up at the conductor. This sign is used in professional symphony orchestras.

With simple tenderness (Key of F major)

Sonatina for Strings

M. CLEMENTI, Op. 36, No. 1
*Transcribed for String Orchestra
by Samuel Applebaum*

Use the martelé stroke on the notes marked with dots. The notes marked with dots and dashes are to be played détaché lancé, which is a smooth stroke with a slight pause after the note has been played.
// The two slanted lines mean that the bow is to be lifted from the string.
o‑o This means that you are to look up at the conductor. This sign is used in professional symphony orchestras.
▫ The small square notes indicate that the finger is to be placed on two strings. This square note is to be stopped by the fingers but not played. It makes it possible to go from one string to another smoothly.

12

13

Moods

BÉLA BÁRTOK
*Transcribed for String Orchestra
by Samuel Applebaum*

- **,** – leave a slight pause for phrasing at each comma (,) with the bow remaining on the string.
- **//** – lift the bow at the slanted lines.
- notes marked with a dot and a dash are to be played détaché lancé —— a smooth stroke with a slight pause between each note.
- Use the martelé stroke on the quarter notes marked with dots. Use the spiccato stroke on the eighth notes marked with dots.

I. Joyful (Canon)

Allegro vivace

II. Sadness

Andante espressivo (♩ = 69)

Copyright © 1967, 1991 (Assigned) CPP/BELWIN, INC.
International Copyright Secured   Made In U.S.A.   All Rights Reserved

III. Mischievous

IV. Remorseful

V. Festive